For Marina

With thanks to those
who have lit up the
path to stillness

Mindfulness is the aware, balanced acceptance of the present experience. It isn't more complicated than that. It is opening to or receiving the present moment, pleasant or unpleasant, just as it is, without either clinging to it or rejecting it.

Sadhguru

Watch, witness. Your body is not you; your mind is not you. You are just a pure witness.

Osho

The present moment is filled with joy and happiness. If you are attentive, you will see it.

Thich Nhat Hanh

The only way to live is by accepting each minute as an unrepeatable miracle.

Tara Brach

The present moment is filled with joy and happiness. If you are attentive, you will see it.

Thich Nhat Hanh

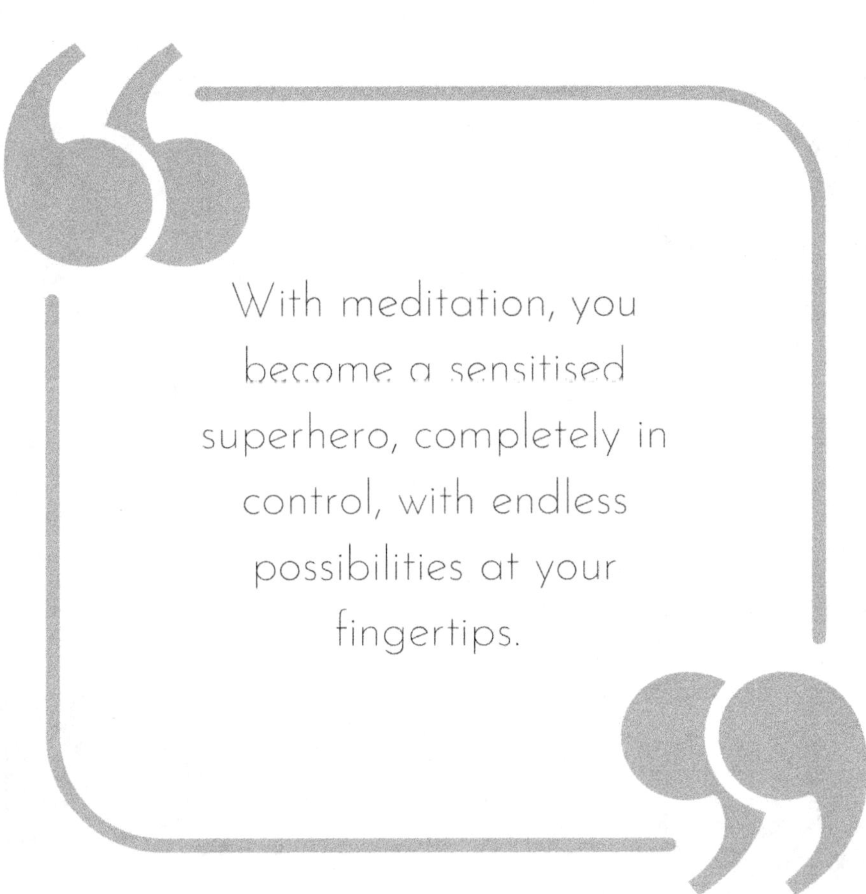

With meditation, you become a sensitised superhero, completely in control, with endless possibilities at your fingertips.

Tara Stiles

As soon as we wish to be happier, we are no longer happy.

Walter Landor

Mindfulness is simply being aware of what is happening right now without wishing it were different.

James Baraz

Mindfulness is the key to unlock the fullness of life. It allows us to awaken to the present moment.

Jack Kornfield

Mindfulness is... enjoying the pleasant without holding on when it changes (which it will); being with the unpleasant without fearing it will always be this way (which it won't).

Ariana Huffington

The best way to capture
moments is to pay attention.
This is how we cultivate
mindfulness.

Jon Kabat-Zinn

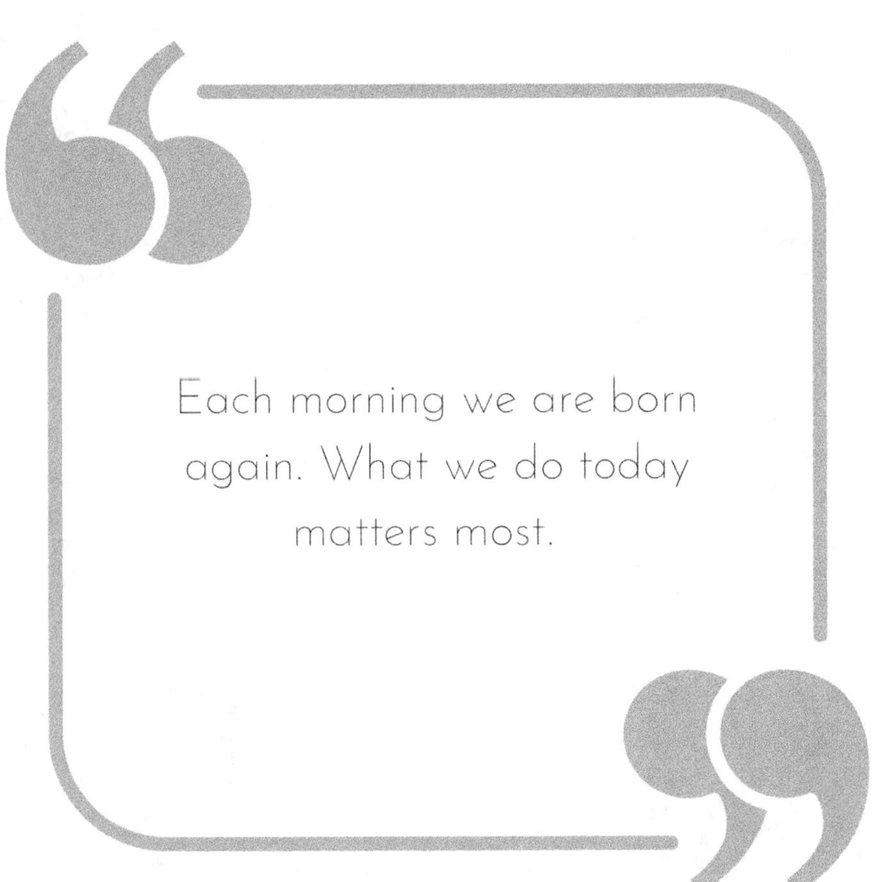

Buddha

Smile, breathe, and go slowly.

Thich Nhat Hanh

He who has freed himself of
the disease of 'tomorrow'
has a chance to attain what
he came here for.

G.I. Gurdji

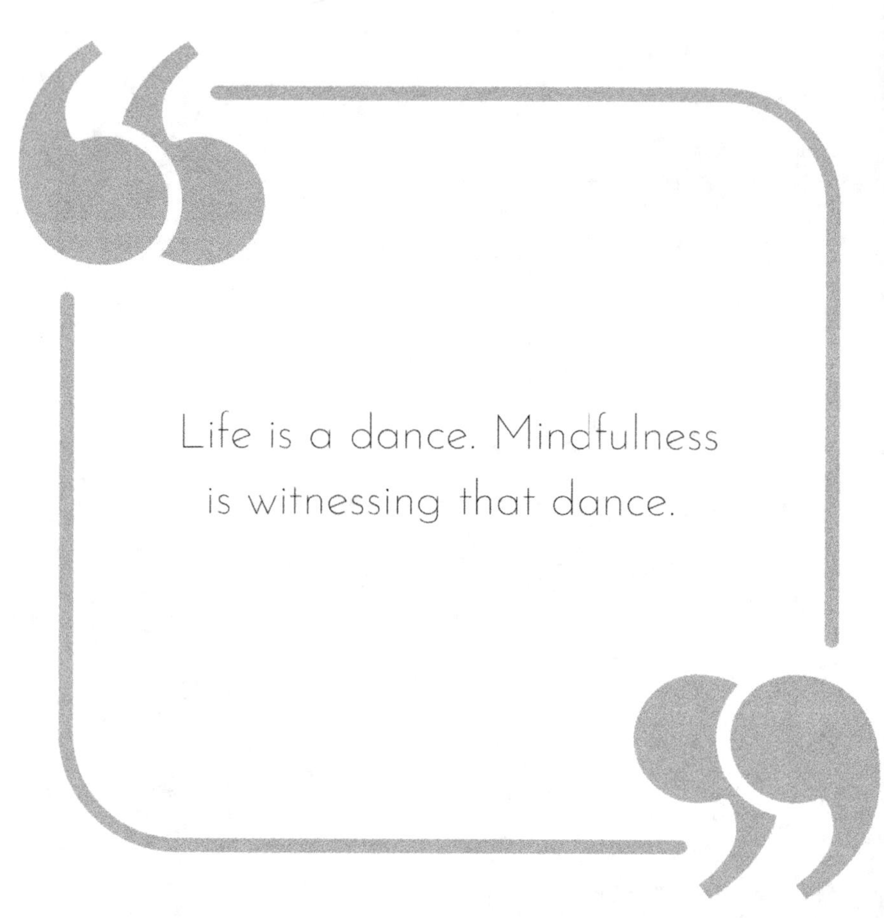

Amit Ray

There is no way to happiness. Happiness is the way.

Thich Nhat Hanh

Drink your tea slowly and reverently, as if it is the axis on which the world earth revolves.

Thich Nhat Hanh

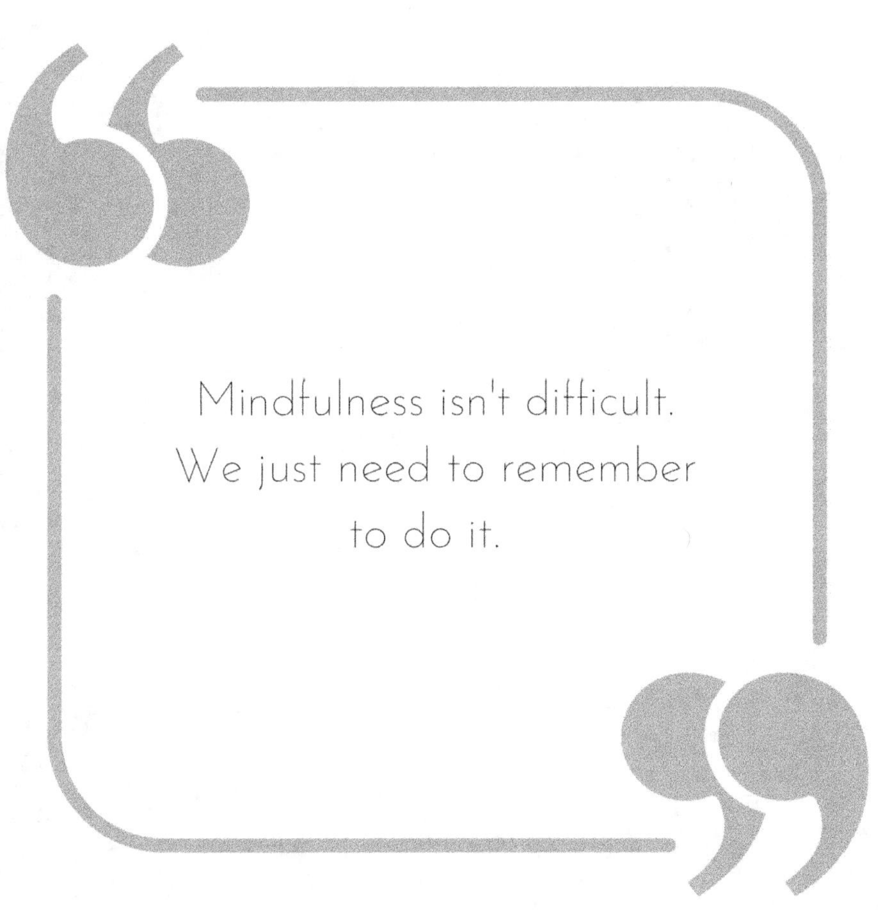

Sharon Salzberg

Meditation is allowing what
is.

Victor Davich

In the midst of movement
and chaos, keep stillness
inside of you.

Deepak Chopra

The present moment is a precious gem. Don't lose it by trying to get somewhere else.

Thich Nhat Hanh

The mind is like water.
When it's turbulent, it's
difficult to see. When it's
calm, everything becomes
clear.

Prasad Mahes

Everything that has a
beginning has an ending.
Make your peace with that
and all will be well.

Jack Kornfield

We realise the importance
of our voices only when we
are silenced.

Malala Yousafzai

Mindfulness isn't about
getting anywhere else; it's
about being where you are
and knowing it.

Jon Kabat-Zinn

The present moment is the
only moment available to
us, and it is the door to all
moments.

Thich Nhat Hanh

The practice of mindfulness
begins in the small, remote
cave of your unconscious mind
and blossoms with the sunlight
of your conscious life, reaching
far beyond the people and
places you can see.

Earl Nightingale

To think in terms of either
pessimism or optimism
oversimplifies the truth. The
problem is to see reality as
it is.

Thich Nhat Hanh

When we do the best we can, we never know what miracle is wrought in our life, or in the life of another.

Helen Keller

Don't believe everything you think. Thoughts are just that —thoughts.

Allan Lokos

You must live in the present,
launch yourself on every
wave, find your eternity in
each moment.

Henry David Thoreau

Mindfulness helps you go home to the present. And every time you go there and recognise a condition of happiness that you have, happiness comes.

Thich Nhat Hanh

The way to live in the present is to remember that 'This too shall pass.' When you experience joy, remembering that and now.

Dani Shapiro

The way in which we think
of ourselves has everything
to do with how our world
see us and how we see
ourselves successfully ,
acknowledged by the world.

Arlene Rankin

In this moment, there is plenty of time. In this moment, you are, precisely as you should be.

Victoria Moran

In the silence between your
thoughts, you'll find peace
and clarity.

Ralph Smart

You don't have to control your thoughts. You just have to stop letting them control you.

Dan Millma

The most precious gift we
can offer others is our
presence. When mindfulness
embraces those we love,
they will bloom like flowers.

Thich Nhat Hanh

One of the most
courageous things you can
do is identify yourself, know
who you are, what you
believe in and where you
want to go.

Sheila Murray Bethel

Awareness is like the sun.
When it shines on things,
they are transformed.

Thich Nhat Hanh

Walk as if you are kissing
the Earth with your feet.

Thich Nhat Hanh

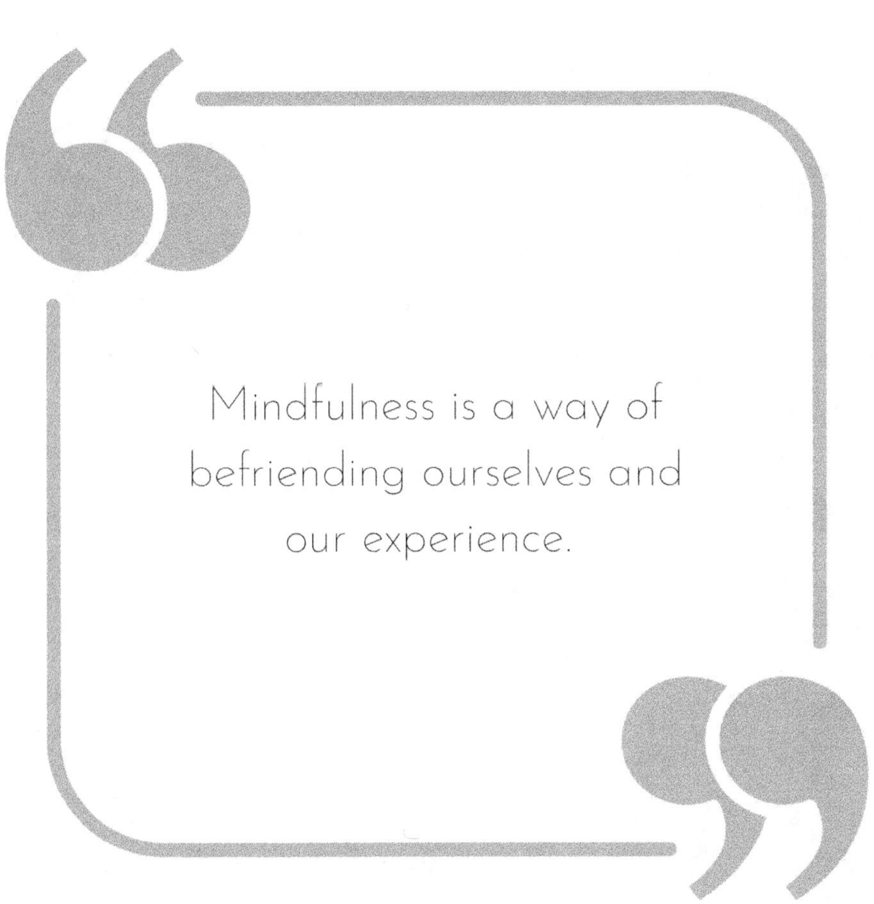

Jon Kabat-Zinn

Life is available only in the
present moment.

Thich Nhat Hanh

Wherever you are, be there
totally.

Eckhart Tolle

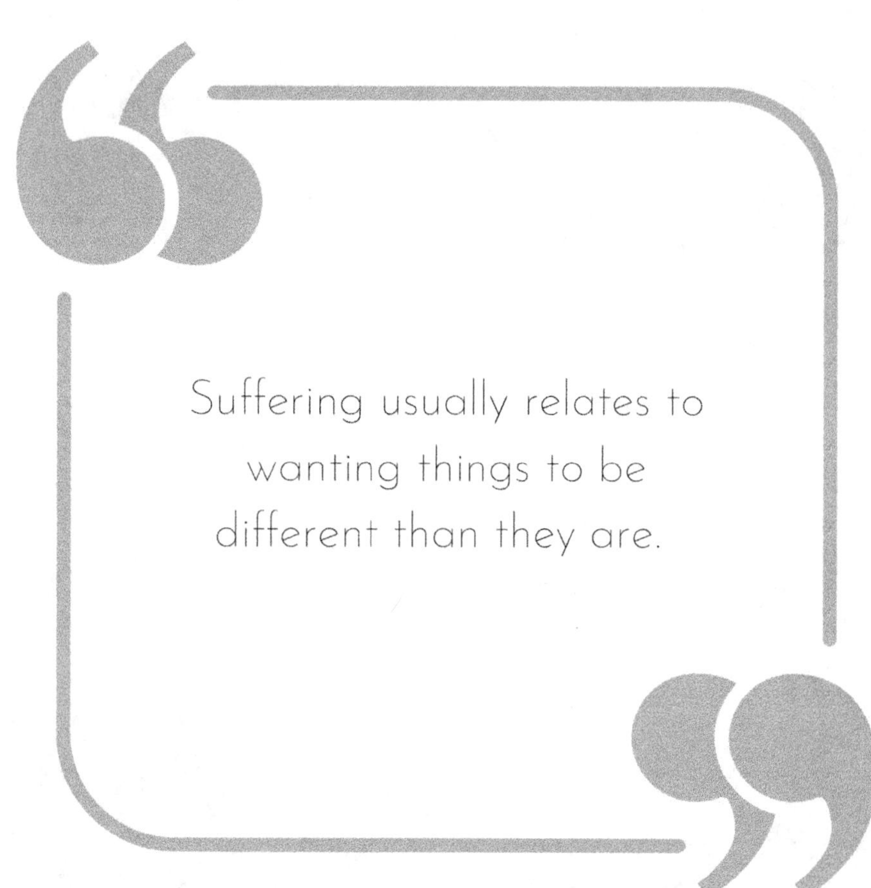

Suffering usually relates to wanting things to be different than they are.

Allan Lokos

Breath is the bridge which connects life to consciousness, which unites your body to your thoughts.

Thich Nhat Hanh

Mediation is a vital way to
purify and quiet the mind,
thus rejuvenating the body.

Deepak Chopra

Remember the blue sky. It
may at times be obscured
by clouds, but it is always
there.

Andy Puddicombe

Meditation is allowing what
is.

Victor Davich

I meditate so that my mind
cannot complicate my life.

Sri Chinmoy

Think about the practice of
meditation as zoning in, as
opposed to spacing out.

Susie Levan

When you're feeling
frazzled, put all of your
attention on the breath. It's
a portal into the present
moment, the best remedy
for stress.

Ellen Barrett

With meditation, you begin
to relax in your seat and just
watch the movie of life.

Ken Wilber

Mindfulness clears the windshield of the mind so that we can see things as they really are.

Travis Eliot

"Paradise is not a place; it's
a state of consciousness.

Sri Chinmoy

If you miss the present moment, you miss your appointment with life. That is very serious!

Thich Nhat Hanh

Worrying is stupid. It's like walking around with an umbrella waiting for it to rain.

Wiz Khalifa

Nature does not hurry, yet everything is accomplished.

Lao Tzu

When you're quiet,
everything settles on the
floor of your mind like
sediment in undisturbed still
water.

Megan Monahan

When you live mindfully,
each breath becomes a
prayer.

Unknown

There is nothing more important to true growth than realising that you are not the voice of the mind— you are the one who hears it.

Michael A. Singer

To understand the
immeasurable, the mind
must be extraordinarily
quiet, still.

Jiddu Krishnamurti

There is no enlightenment
outside of daily life.

Thich Nhat Hanh

A mind is like a parachute.
It doesn't work if it isn't
open.

Frank Zappa

The moment you start
watching the thinker, a
higher level of consciousness
becomes activated.

Eckhart Tolle

If you want to conquer the anxiety of life, live in the moment, live in the breath.

Amit Ray

The moment one gives close
attention to anything, even
a blade of grass, it becomes
a mysterious, awesome,
indescribably magnificent
world in itself.

Henry Miller

Do not dwell in the past, do
not dream of the future,
concentrate the mind on the
present moment.

Buddha

If you are depressed, you are living in the past. If you are anxious, you are living in the future. If you are at peace, you are living in the present.

Lao Tzu

The present moment is the
only time over which we
have dominion.

Thich Nhat Hanh

Mindfulness is the ultimate weapon for the modern warrior.

Tom Evans

The real meditation is how
you live your life.

Jon Kabat-Zinn

The past has no power over
the present moment.

Eckhart Tolle

When you realize nothing is
lacking, the whole world
belongs to you.

Lao Tzu

As you walk and eat and travel, be where you are. Otherwise, you will miss most of your life.

Buddha

The present moment is a
powerful goddess.

Johann Wolfgang von
Goethe

The present moment is all
you ever have.

Eckhart Tolle

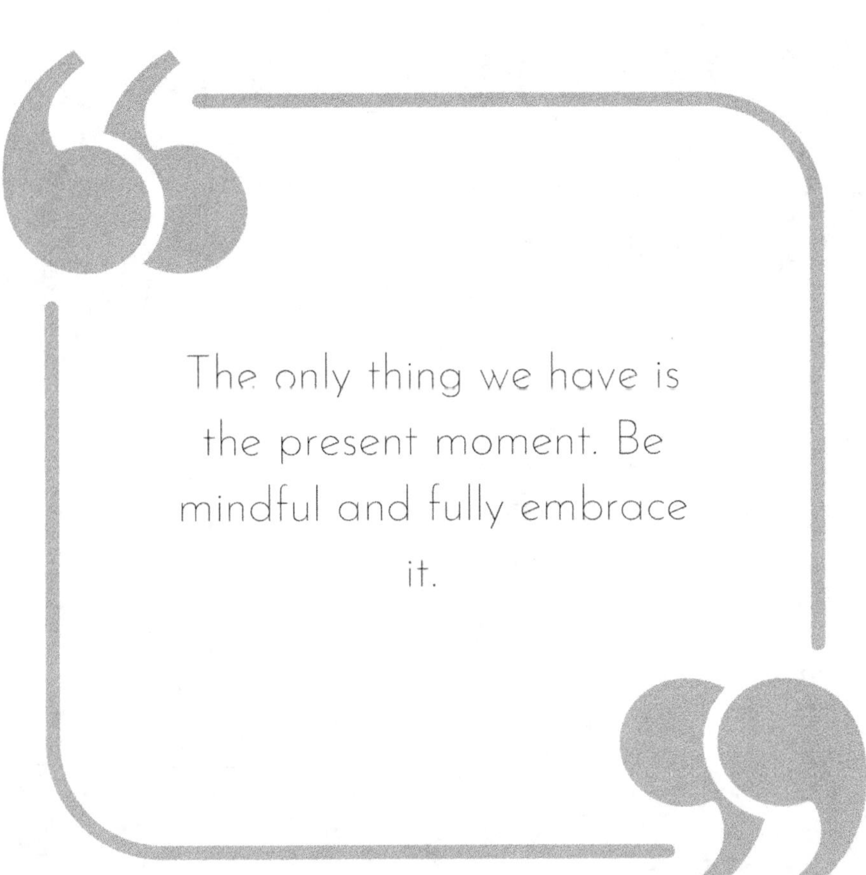

Thich Nhat Hanh

In the present moment, life
is as perfect as it can be.

Donna Fargo

The quieter you become, the
more you can hear.

Ram Dass

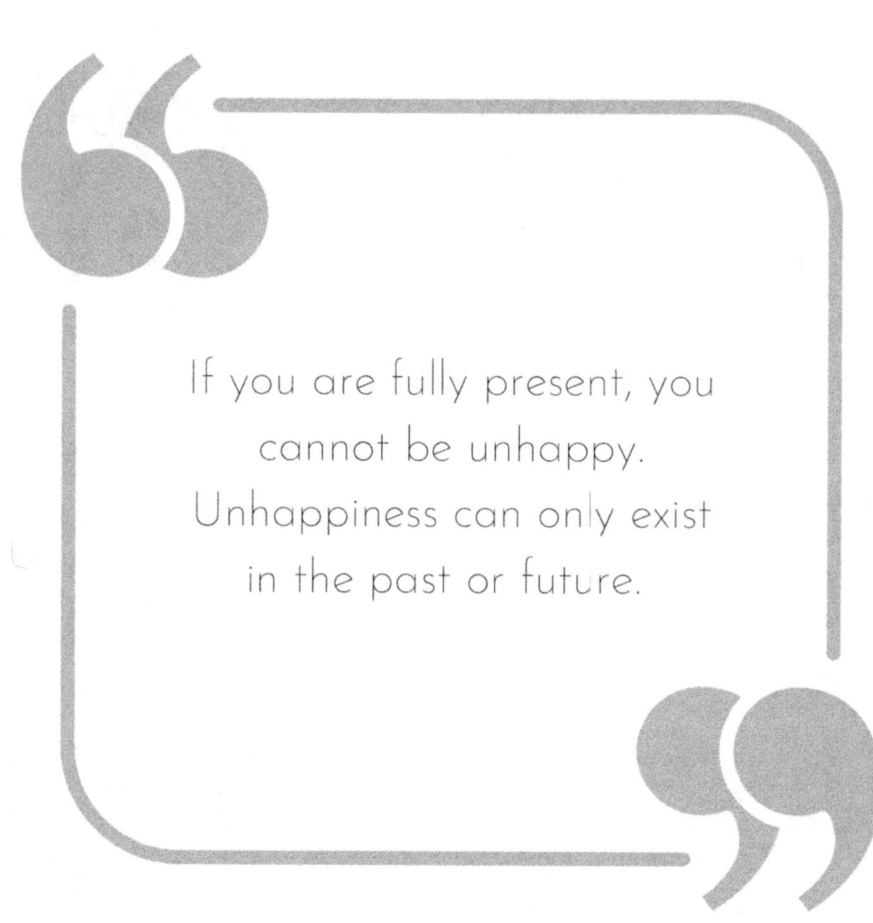

Eckhart Tolle

There is a calmness to a life
lived in gratitude, a quiet
joy.

Ralph H. Blum

When you pay attention to
boredom, it gets
unbelievably interesting.

Jon Kabat-Zinn

The mind is everything.
What you think you
become.

Buddha

You can't stop the waves,
but you can learn to surf.

Jon Kabat-Zinn

Mindfulness, the Root of Happiness.

Joseph Goldstein

When you walk, just walk.
When you eat, just eat.

Zen Proverb

The present moment is the
only moment where life can
be found.

Eckhart Tolle

Let go of your mind and then be mindful. Close your ears and listen!

Rumi

In the end, just three things matter: How well we have lived. How well we have loved. How well we have learned to let go.

Jack Kornfield

Stop acting as if life is a rehearsal. Live this day as if it were your last. The past is over and gone. The future is not guaranteed.

Wayne Dyer

The real voyage of
discovery consists not in
seeking out new landscapes
but in having new eyes.

Marcel Proust

In the present moment,
there is infinite possibility.

Victoria Moran

Reality is only an agreement
– today is always today.

Zen Proverb

Your attention is your most
valuable asset. Be mindful
of how you spend it.

R. D. Laing

Maya Angelou

The perfect moment is this
one.

Jon Kabat-Zinn

Savour the present moment. It holds the key to true happiness.

Unknown

Few of us ever live in the present. We are forever anticipating what is to come or remembering what has gone.

Louis L'Amour

The beauty of mindfulness is that it doesn't ask you to change anything. It simply asks you to be aware.

Unknown

Breathe out unwanted thoughts with your exhale and re-focus your attention directly on what is important right now, at this moment.

Amit Ray

Awareness is the greatest
agent for change.

Eckhart Tolle

Be present. Be mindful. Be alive in this moment.

Unknown

Breathe deeply. Embrace the present moment. Find peace within.

Unknown

Raise your words, not your
voice. It is rain that grows
flowers, not thunder.

Rumi

In the stillness of the present
moment, you will find the
answers you seek.

Use every distraction as an object of meditation and they cease to be distractions.

Mingyur Rinpoche

If it's out of your hands, it deserves freedom from your mind too.

Ivan Nuru

Mindfulness is a pause – the space between stimulus and response: that's where choice lies.

Tara Brach

The present time has one advantage over every other – it is our own.

Charles Caleb Colton

Mindfulness is deliberately paying full attention to what is happening around you– in your body, heart, and mind. Mindfulness is awareness without criticism or judgment.

Jan Chozen Bays

In the present moment,
everything is possible.

Unknown

Mindfulness is the gateway
to self-discovery and
personal growth.

Unknown

I meditate regularly. It's a way to step back and see the big picture, focus on the things that are most important, and make decisions with clarity.

Bill Gates

When you truly know
yourself, you don't try to
impress people anymore.
One way to know yourself is
to meditate.

Maxime Lagace

Be you, love you. All ways, always.

Alexandra Elle

James Allen

Mindfulness is the practice
of being fully engaged in
the present moment.

Unknown

If you want others to be
happy, practice compassion.
If you want to be happy,
practice compassion.

Dalai Lama

Whatever is fluid, soft, and yielding will overcome whatever is rigid and hard. What is soft is strong.

Lao Tzu

The present moment is the
only time when you can
truly be alive.

Unknown

There are no secrets, no
formulas. It's just a matter
of looking carefully.

Colin Poole

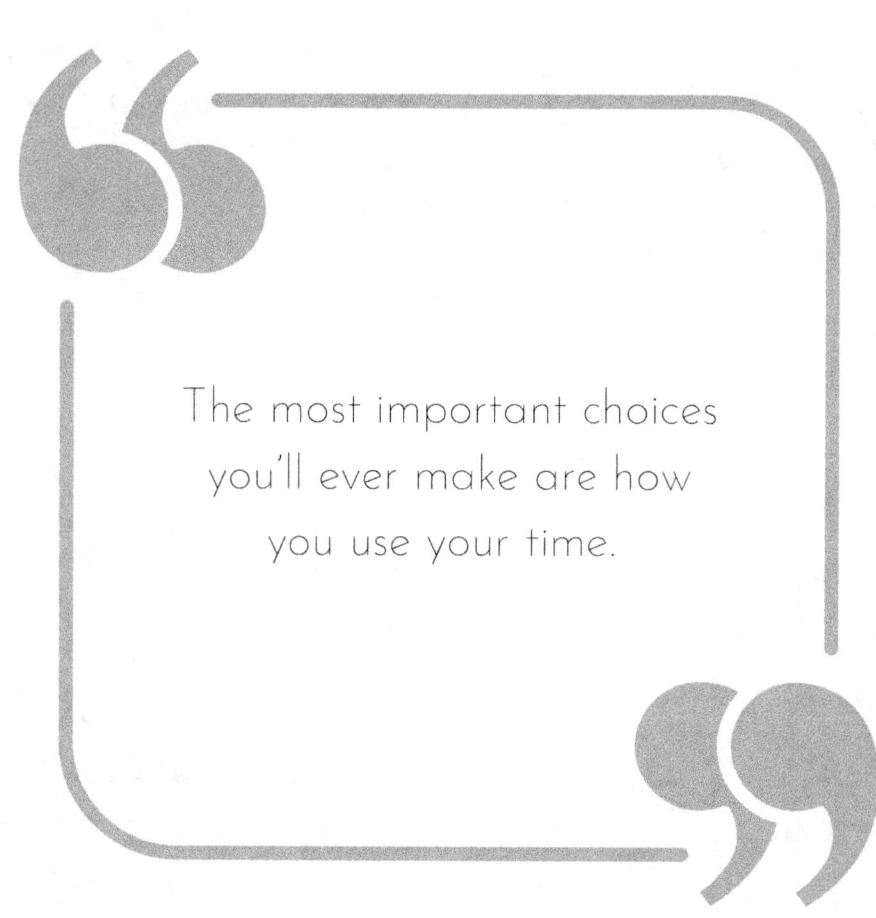

David Kekich

When meditation is
mastered, the mind is
unwavering like the flame of
a candle in a windless place.

Bhagavad Gita

Embrace the present
moment with open arms. It
holds the key to your
happiness.

Unknown

Nowhere can man find a quieter or more untroubled retreat than in his own soul.

Marcus Aurelius

The power of mindfulness
lies in its ability to bring you
back to the present
moment.

Unknown

Your calm mind is the ultimate weapon against your challenges. So relax.

Bryant McGill

Meditation means dissolving
the invisible walls that
unawareness has built.

Sadhguru

Mindfulness is the antidote
to stress and anxiety. It
brings you back to the here
and now.

Unknown

Quiet the mind, and the
soul will speak.

Ma Jaya Sati Bhagavati

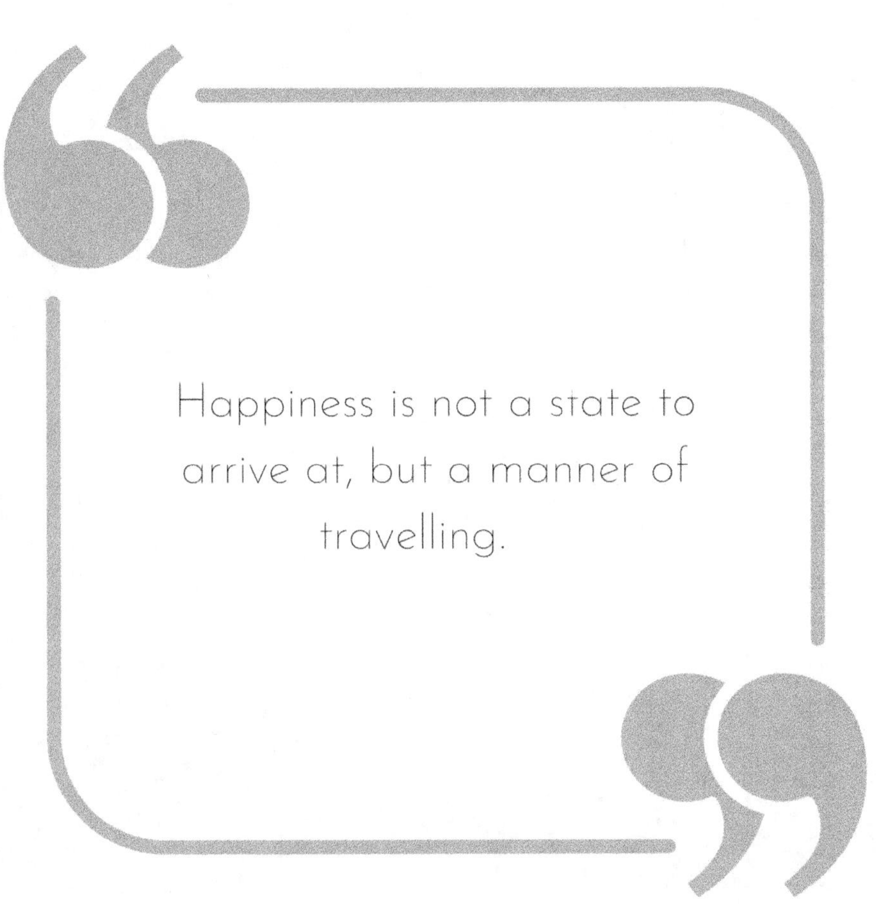

Margaret Lee Runbeck

When you own your breath,
nobody can steal your
peace.

Unknown

The present moment is a
precious jewel. Hold it
gently in your hands.

Unknown

The more you are
motivated by love, the more
fearless and free your
actions will be.

Dalai Lama

Every emotion is connected with the breath. If you change the breath, change the rhythm, you can change the emotion.

Sri Sri Ravi Shankar

Meditation is all about the pursuit of nothingness. It's like the ultimate rest. It's better than the best sleep you've ever had. It's a quieting of the mind.

Hugh Jackman

Learn to slow down. Get lost intentionally. Observe how you judge both yourself and those around you.

Tim Ferriss

Suffering is due to our disconnection with the inner soul. Meditation is establishing that connection.

Amit Ray

Gratitude turns what we
have into enough.

Aesop

Whatever state I am in, I
see it as a state of mind to
be accepted as it is.

Nisargadatta Maharaj

Be thankful for what you have; you'll end up having more. If you concentrate on what you don't have, you will never, ever have enough.

Oprah Winfrey

In the present moment, you
can find peace, joy, and
clarity.

Unknown

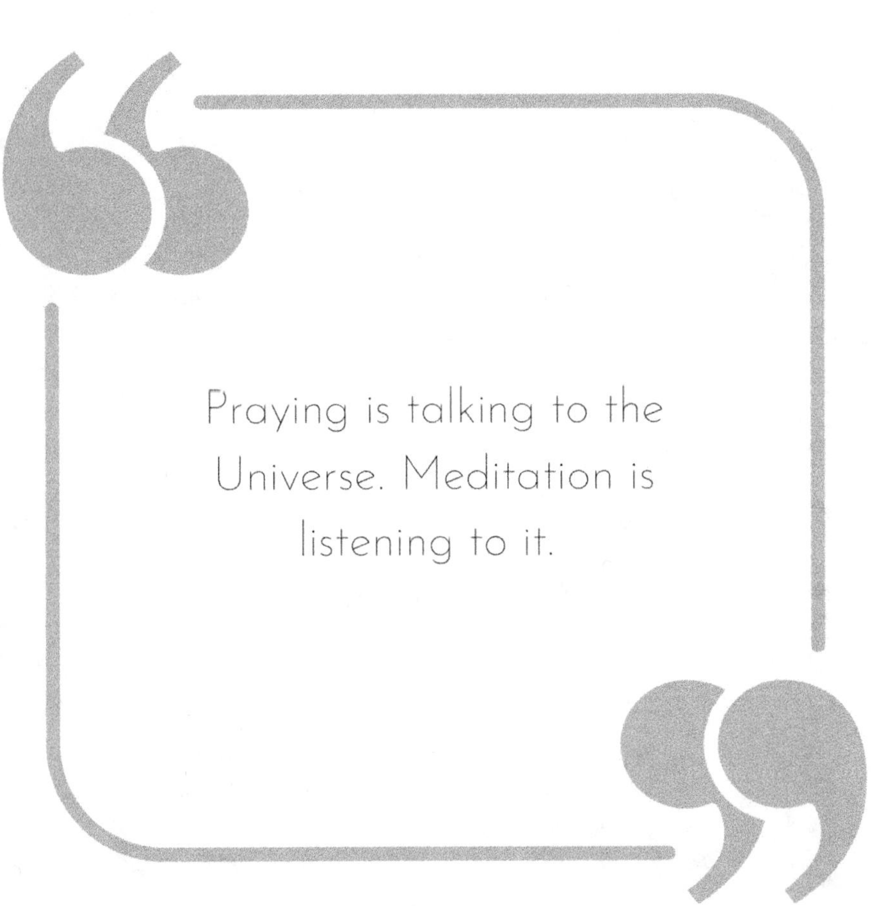

Paulo Coelho

In our times, it is radical to choose to sit still and be silent, to resist an identity of busyness, ceaseless motion, and noise, and to reclaim our sanity and humanity by coming home to ourselves.

Sumi Loundon Kim

I believe that mindfulness can help you find inner peace and happiness. It's a journey, but it's worth it.

Madonna

In moments of quiet reflection,
I am filled with a sense of
gratitude for the journey I
have travelled, for the people I
have known, and for the rich
tapestry of experiences that
have shaped me.

Nelson Mandela

The present moment is the doorway to your true self.

Unknown

To really do nothing, with perfection, is as difficult as doing everything.

Alan Watts

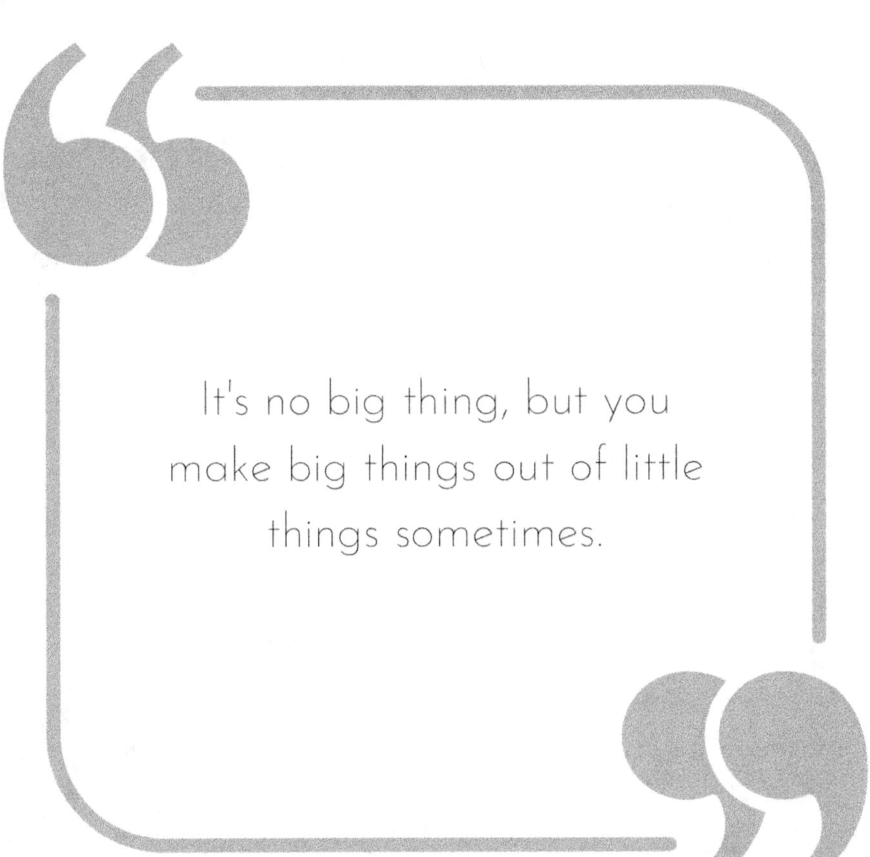

It's no big thing, but you make big things out of little things sometimes.

Robert Duvall

Mindfulness is a mental
activity that in due course
eliminates all suffering.

Ayya Khema

In the present moment, you
can let go of the past and
create a brighter future.

Unknown

Dalai Lama

You have a treasure within you that is infinitely greater than anything the world can offer.

Eckhart Tolle

Mindfulness isn't about getting rid of your thoughts. It's about learning to be at ease with them.

Sharon Salzberg

Be present in the moment,
for it holds the potential for
infinite possibilities.

Unknown

We need to accept that we won't always make the right decisions, that we'll screw up royally sometimes - understanding that failure is not the opposite of success, it's part of success.

Ariana Huffington

Mindfulness is the miracle
by which we master and
restore ourselves.

Thich Nhat Hanh

In the present moment, you
have the power to create
positive change.

Unknown

Rejoicing in ordinary things
is not sentimental or trite. It
actually takes guts.

Pema Chödrön

When you live mindfully, each step becomes a meditation.

Unknown

Wisdom comes with the ability to be still. Just look and listen. No more is needed.

Eckhart Tolle

We have only now, only this
single eternal moment
opening and unfolding
before us, day and night.

Jack Kornfield

The future is something
which everyone reaches at
the rate of sixty minutes an
hour, whatever he does,
whoever he is.

C.S. Lewis

The present moment is a gift. That's why they call it the present.

Unknown

Meditation practice isn't about trying to throw ourselves away and become something better. It's about befriending who we are already.

Pema Chödrön

Be kind whenever possible.
It is always possible.

Dalai Lama

Nature does not hurry, yet
everything is accomplished.

Lao Tzu

Mindfulness means being
awake. It means knowing
what you are doing.

Jon Kabat-Zinn

In the present moment, you
can find peace, happiness,
and fulfilment.

Unknown

I start every day with a meditation. It puts me in the right mindset to tackle everything I need to do that day.

Katy Perry

You are more than just your
mind. You are more than
just your habits. You are
more than just your
preferences. You're a level
of awareness.

Naval Ravikant

Observe the space between
your thoughts, then observe
the observer.

Hamilton Boudreaux

The present moment is a canvas. Paint it with mindfulness and love.

Unknown

Meditation is a way for me
to be calm and centered
and to get that balance
back, especially when things
are hectic.

Jennifer Aniston

When you are fully present,
you can connect deeply with
yourself and others.

Unknown

Cultivating a generous spirit
starts with mindfulness.
Mindfulness, simply stated,
means paying attention to
what is happening; it's about
what is really going on.

Nell Newman

Be curious, not judgmental.

Walt Whitman

Meditation is not evasion; it is a serene encounter with reality.

Thich Nhat Hanh

Take time to deliberate; but when the time for action arrives, stop thinking and go in.

Andrew Jackson

Paradise is not a place, it's
a state of consciousness.

Sri Chinmoy

Surrender to what is. Let go
of what was. Have faith in
what will be.

Sonia Ricotti

You see, but you do not observe.

Arthur Conan Doyle

Almost everything will work
again if you unplug it for a
few minutes ... including you.

Anne Lamott

The habit of spending nearly every waking moment lost in thought leaves us at the mercy of whatever our thoughts happen to be. Meditation is a way of breaking this spell.

Sam Harris

If you aren't in the moment, you are either looking forward to uncertainty, or back to pain and regret.

Jim Carrey

Meditation is all about
connecting with your soul.

Deepak Chopra

Your goal is not to battle
with the mind, but to witness
the mind.

Swami Muktananda

There is something
wonderfully bold and
liberating about saying yes
to our entire imperfect and
messy life.

Tara Brach

Respond; don't react. Listen; don't talk. Think; don't assume.

Raji Lukkoor

Meditation brings wisdom;
lack of meditation leaves
ignorance. Know well what
leads you forward and what
hold you back, and choose
the path that leads to
wisdom.

Buddha

Meditation is freedom from thought and a movement in the ecstasy of truth. Meditation is an explosion of intelligence.

Jiddu Krishnamurti

Step outside for a while –
calm your mind. It is better
to hug a tree than to bang
your head against a wall
continually.

Rasheed Ogunlaru

Meditation is to be aware of every thought and of every feeling, never to say it is right or wrong but just to watch it and move with it.

Jiddu Krishnamurti

Mindful and creative, a child who has neither a past, nor examples to follow, nor value judgments, simply lives, speaks and plays in freedom.

Arnaud Desjardins

Meditation could be said to
be the Art of Simplicity:
simply sitting, simply
breathing and simply being.

Dilgo Khyentse
Rinpoche

Meditation is a death - death of all that you are now. Of course there will be a resurrection, but that will be a totally new, fresh original being which you are not even aware is hidden in you.

Osho

This is the real secret of life
— to be completely
engaged with what you are
doing in the here and now.
And instead of calling it
work, realize it is play.

Alan Watts

Happiness is your nature. It
is not wrong to desire it.
What is wrong is seeking it
outside when it is inside.

Ramana Maharshi

What would it be like if I could accept life – accept this moment – exactly as it is?

Tara Brach

If you concentrate on finding whatever is good in every situation, you will discover that your life will suddenly be filled with gratitude, a feeling that nurtures the soul.

Rabbi Harold Kushner

Every time we ponder a thought, act on an impulse, or dwell on a desire, we are setting in motion a cause that will have a future effect. Mindfulness enables us to choose wisely.

Tamara Levitt

Whatever anyone does or
says, I must be emerald and
keep my colour.

Marcus Aurelius

Restore your attention or bring it to a new level by dramatically slowing down whatever you're doing.

Sharon Salzberg

Don't let life harden your
heart.

Pema Chödrön

Meditation is not spacing-out or running away. In fact, it is being totally honest with ourselves.

Kathleen McDonald

Look past your thoughts, so
you may drink the pure
nectar of This Moment.

Rumi

Becoming awake involves seeing our confusion more clearly.

Chogyam Trungpa

When you focus on the
good, the good gets better.

Abraham Hicks

Be present. Be mindful. Be grateful for the gift of life.

Unknown

Mindfulness is the bridge
that connects you to the
beauty and wonder of life.

Unknown

The present moment is
where life happens.
Embrace it fully.

Unknown

You cannot breathe deeply
and worry at the same time.

Sonia Choquette

You are the sky. Everything
else is just the weather.

Pema Chodron

All of man's difficulties are caused by his inability to sit, quietly, in a room by himself.

Blaise Pascal

When you are mindful, you can appreciate the simple joys and miracles of everyday life.

Unknown

The key to growth is the introduction of higher dimensions of consciousness into our awareness.

Lao Tzu

The best way to take care
of the future is to take care
of the present moment.

Thich Nhat Hanh

In the present moment, you
can let go of worries and
find peace.

Unknown

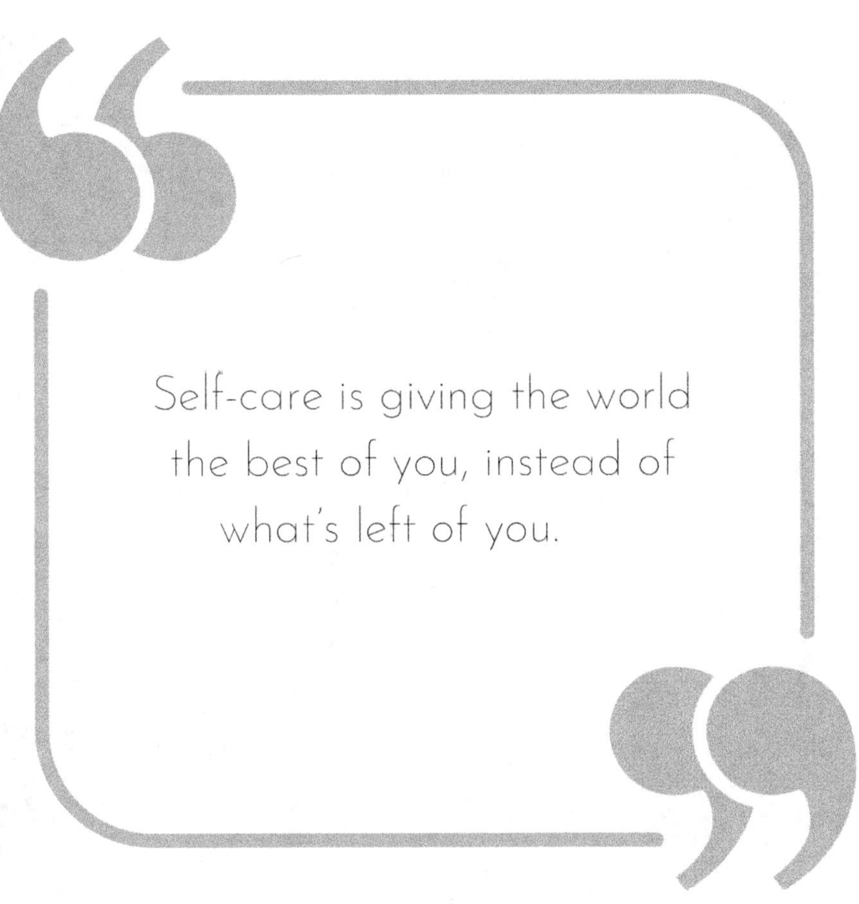

Self-care is giving the world
the best of you, instead of
what's left of you.

Katie Reed

The still waters of a lake reflect the beauty around it. When the mind is still, the beauty of the self is reflected.

Vanda Scaravelli

There's only one reason why you're not experiencing bliss at this present moment, and it's because you're thinking or focusing on what you don't have…. But, right now you have everything you need to be in bliss.

Anthony de Mello

The present moment is a treasure chest. Open it with mindfulness and curiosity.

Unknown

Some of the greatest battles
will be fought within the
silent chambers of your own
soul.

Ezra Taft

Your vision will become clear only when you look into your heart. Who looks outside, dreams. Who looks inside, awakens.

Carl Jung

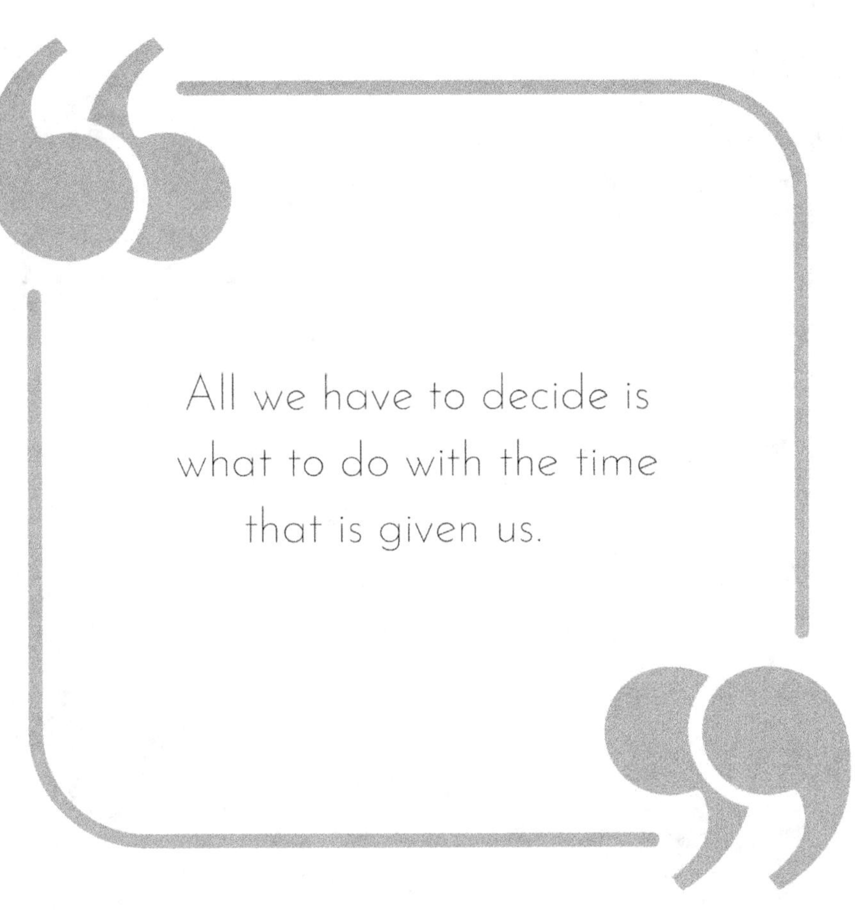

All we have to decide is
what to do with the time
that is given us.

J.R.R. Tolkien

Mindfulness has made me calmer, more peaceful, and more in tune with what I need to be doing at any given moment.

Lady Gaga

We should always allow
some time to elapse, for
time discloses the truth.

Seneca

Mindfulness is the practice
of being fully present and
alive in the here and now.

Unknown

There are only two ways to live your life. One is as though nothing is a miracle. The other is as though everything is a miracle.

Albert Einstein

In the present moment, you
can find inner peace and
serenity.

Unknown

Mindfulness gives you time.
Time gives you choices.
Choices, skillfully made, lead
to freedom.

Bhante Henepola
Gunaratana

Three things can not hide
for long: the Moon, the Sun
and the Truth.

Buddha

Open the window of your
mind. Allow the fresh air,
new lights, and new truths
to enter.

Amit Ray

Through meditation, the
higher self is experienced.

Bhagavad Gita

It's not what you look at
that matters, it's what you
see.

Henry David Thoreau

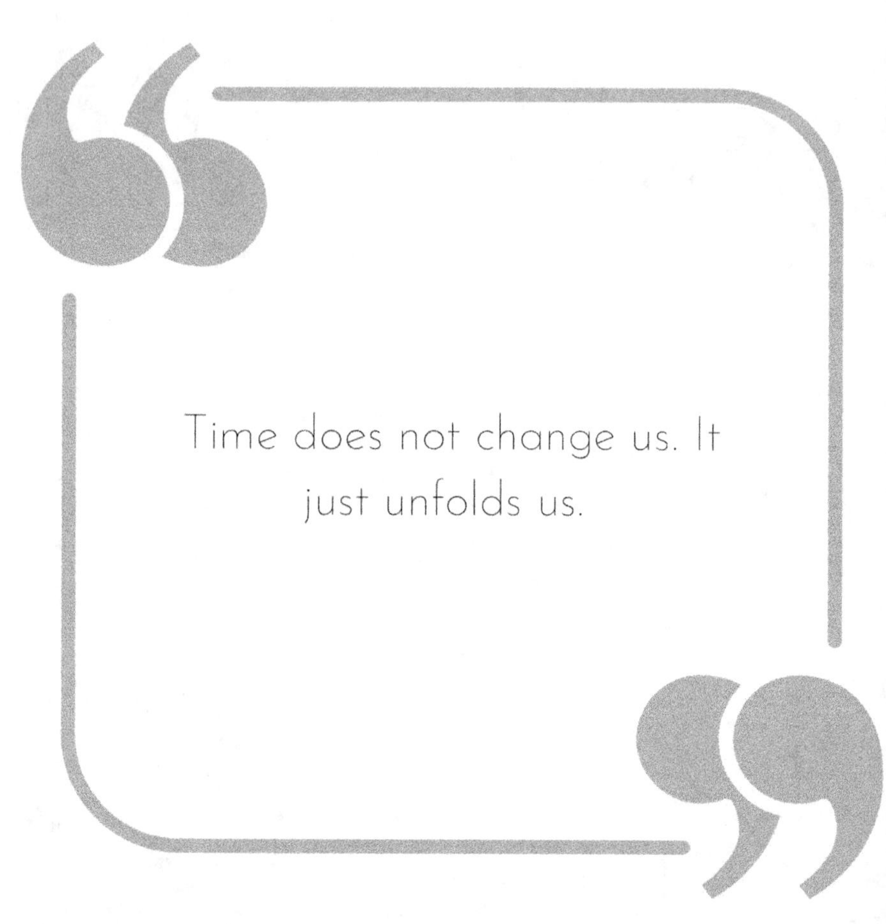

Time does not change us. It just unfolds us.

Max Frisch

237

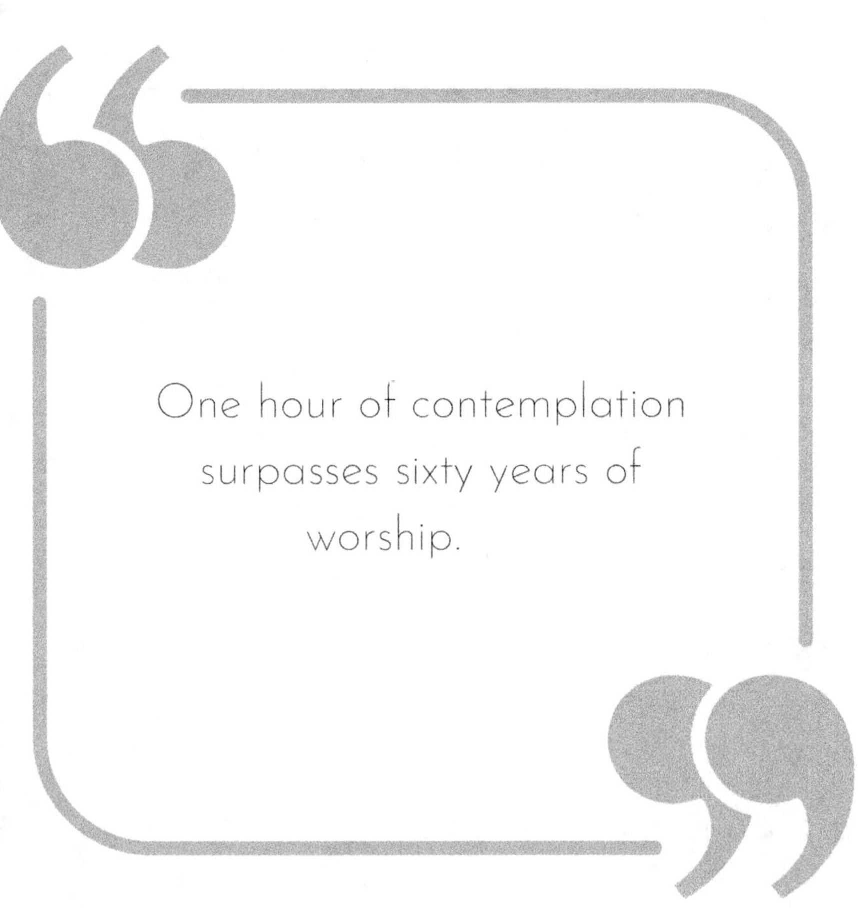

One hour of contemplation surpasses sixty years of worship.

Muhammad

Gratitude and attitude are
not challenges, they are
choices.

Robert Braathe

Nothing is worth more than this day. You cannot relive yesterday. Tomorrow is still beyond your reach.

Johann Wolfgang von Goethe

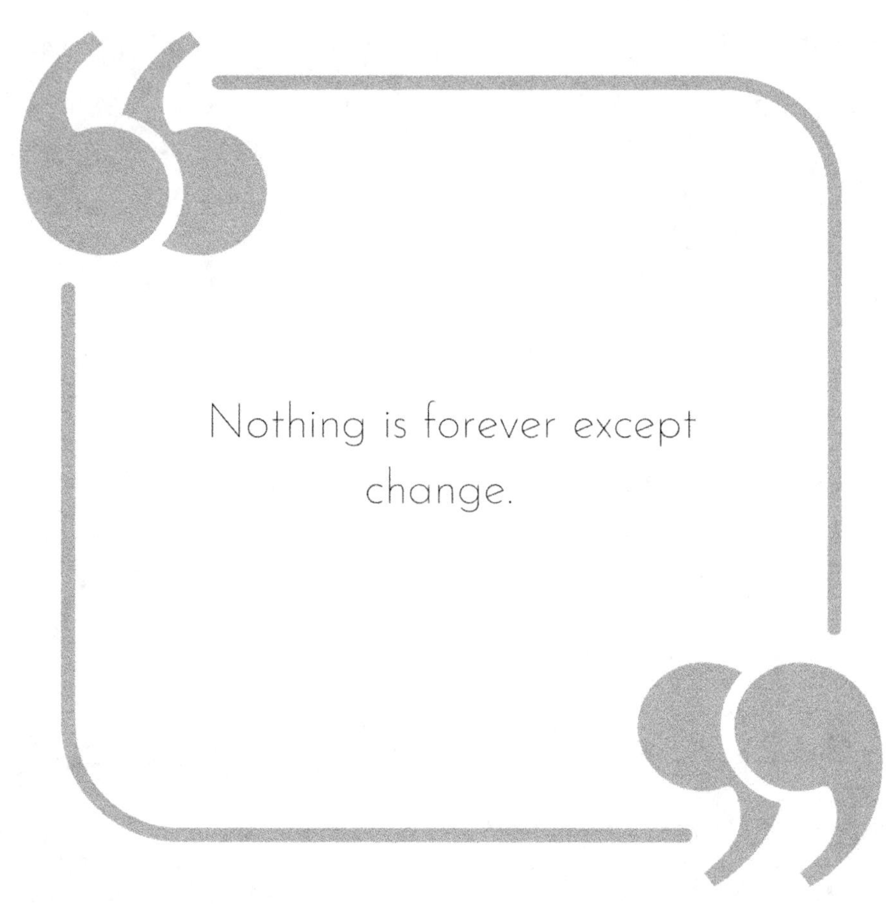

Nothing is forever except change.

Buddha

Wisdom says we are nothing. Love says we are everything. Between these two our life flows.

Jack Kornfield

Yesterday is history.
Tomorrow is a mystery.
Today is a gift. That is why
it is called the present.

Alice Morse Earle

Just when you feel you have no time to relax, know this is the moment you most need to relax.

Matt Haig

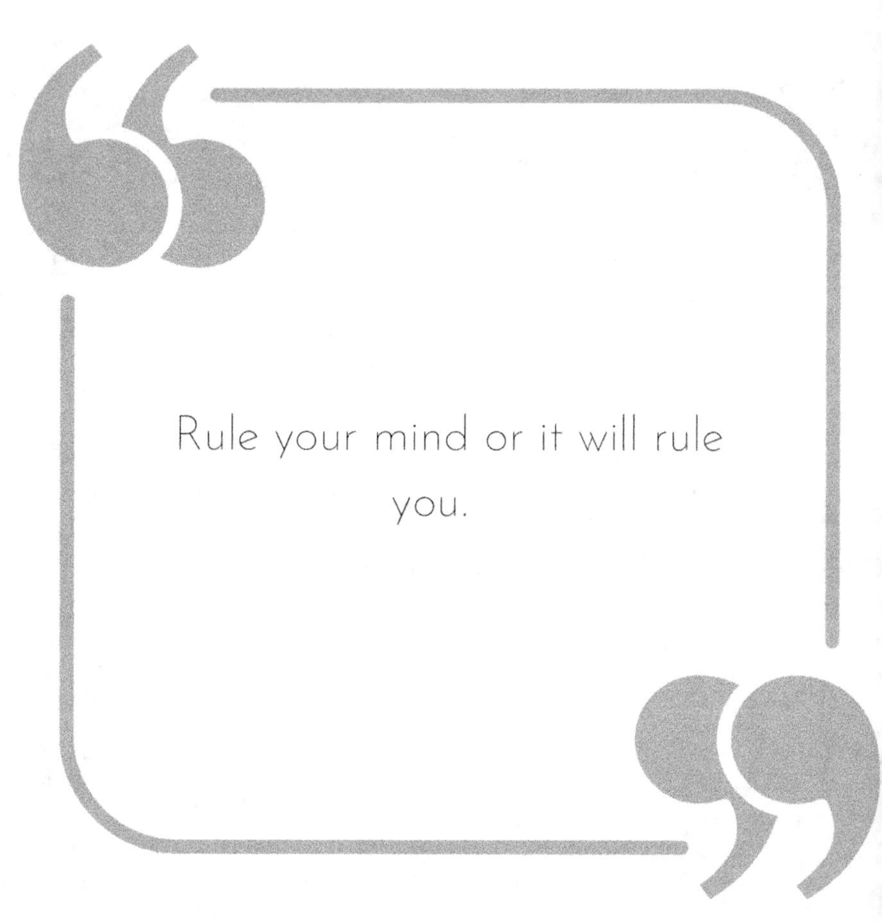

Rule your mind or it will rule
you.

Buddha

A few simple tips for life:
feet on the ground, head to
the skies, heart open...quiet
mind.

Rasheed Ogunlaru

With our thoughts we make
the world.

Buddha

It is never too late to turn
on the light.

Sharon Salzberg

The art of peaceful living
comes down to living
compassionately and wisely.

Allen Lokos

Looking at beauty in the world, is the first step of purifying the mind.

Amit Ray

Time does not pass; it continues.

Marty Rubin

Listen to silence. It has so
much to say.

Rumi

Tea is an act complete in its simplicity. When I drink tea, there is only me and the tea. The rest of the world dissolves.

Thich Nhat Hanh

Be yourself. Everyone else is
already taken.

Oscar Wilde

If the problem can be solved why worry? If the problem cannot be solved worrying will do you no good.

Buddha

Meditation is the action of
silence.

Jiddu Krishnamurti

Just as a snake sheds its
skin, we must shed our past
over and over again.

Buddha

The mind is just like a
muscle – the more you
exercise it, the stronger it
gets and the more it can
expand.

Idowu Koyenikan

Training your mind to be in the present moment is the number one key to making healthier choices.

Susan Albers

Like many of you, I was
concerned about going into
the world and doing
something bigger than myself.
Until someones marter than
myself made me realize that
there is nothing bigger than
myself.

Jim Carrey

That way of being 'still' with ourselves – coming back to the centre and recognising that something is more important than you – it's more important than the work you are doing, brings a kind of energy, an intention that we have never had before.

Oprah Winfrey

Meditation is a lifelong gift.
It's something you can call
on at any time.

Paul McCartney

Life gives you plenty of time
to do whatever you want to
do if you stay in the present
moment.

Deepak Chopra

Treat everyone you meet as
if they were you.

Doug Dillon

In a world deluged by
irrelevant information,
clarity is power.

Yuval Noah Harari

Eric Schmidt

Breath is the finest gift of
nature. Be grateful for this
wonderful gift.

Amit Ray

The things that matter most
in our lives are not fantastic
or grand. They are moments
when we touch one another.

Jack Kornfield

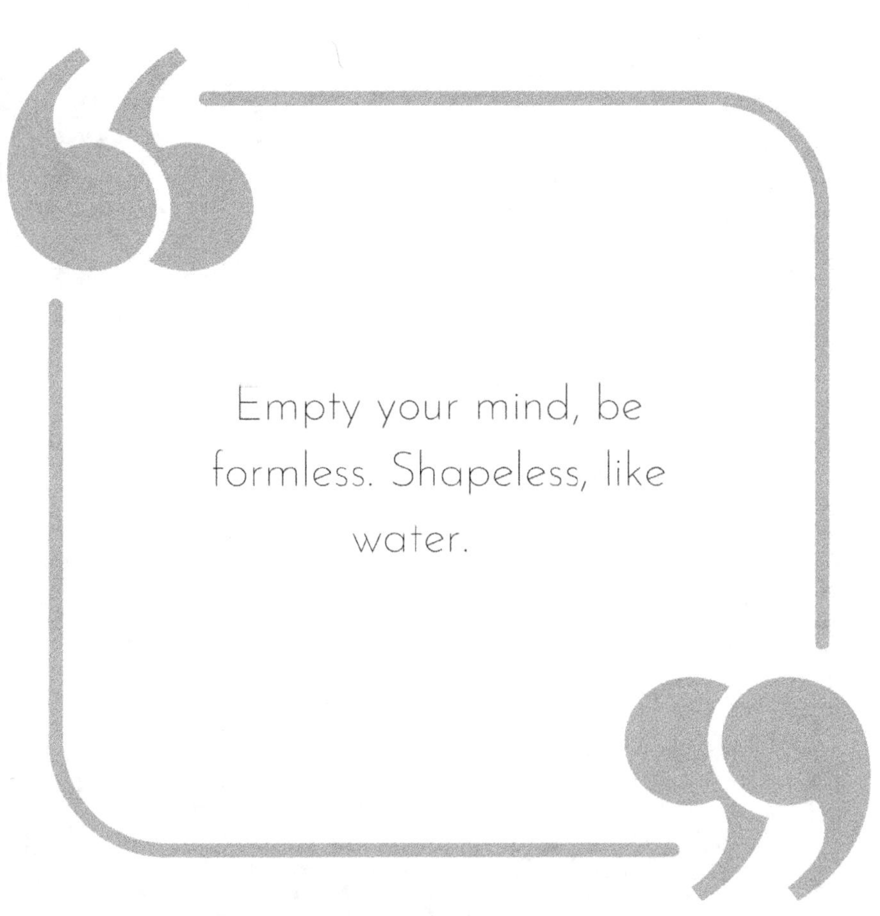

Bruce Lee

The best cure for the body
is a quiet mind.

Napoleon Bonaparte

Breathe and let be.

Jon Kabat-Zinn

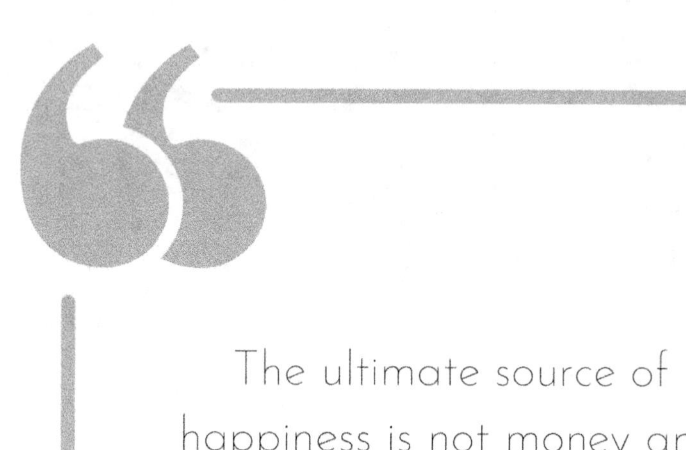

The ultimate source of happiness is not money and power, but warm-heartedness.

Dalai Lama

If you are facing in the right
direction, all you need to do
is keep on walking.

Buddha

When you bow, you should just bow; when you sit, you should just sit; when you eat, you should just eat.

Shunryu Suzuki

Time has a wonderful way of showing us what really matters.

Margaret Peters

Courage doesn't mean you don't get afraid. Courage means you don't let fear stop you.

Bethany Hamilton

How you look at it is pretty
much how you'll see it.

Rasheed Ogunlaru

Without forgiveness, there's
no future.

Desmond Tutu

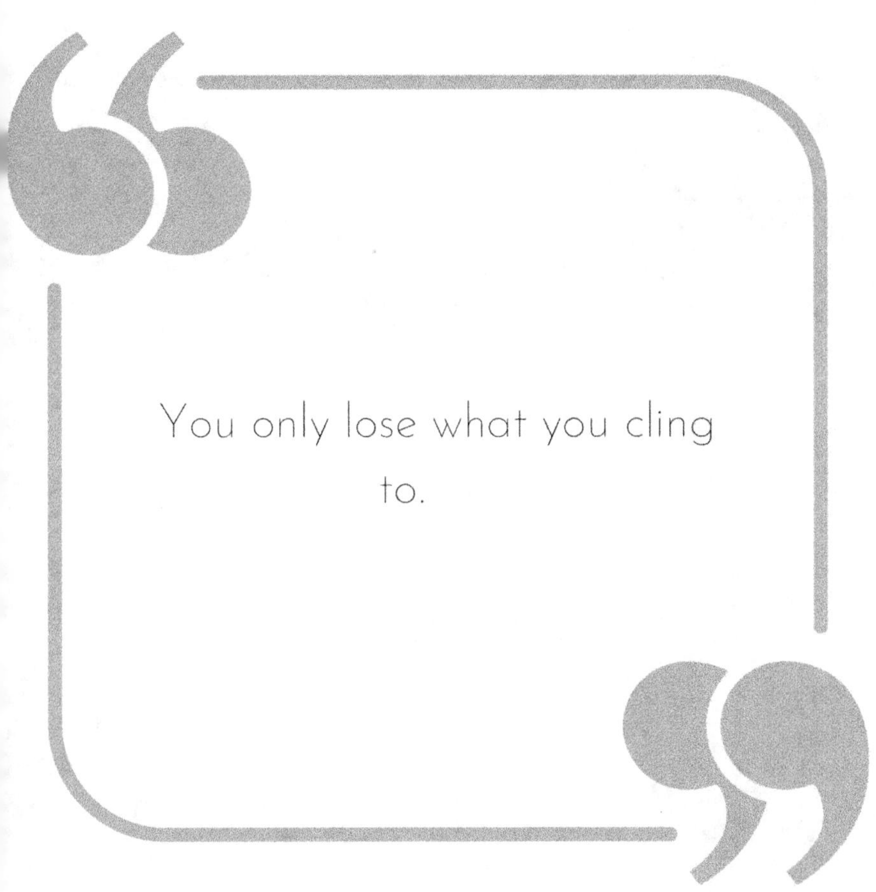

You only lose what you cling
to.

Buddha

The essence of bravery is
being without self-deception.

Pema Chodron

You must be completely
awake in the present to
enjoy the tea.

Thich Nhat Hanh

One who is patient glows
with an inner radiance.

Allan Lokos

Change your thoughts and
you change your world.

Norman Vincent Peale

That's life: starting over, one breath at a time.

Sharon Salzberg

The Way is not in the sky,
the Way is in the heart.

Buddha

Reading makes a full man,
meditation a profound man,
discourse a clear man.

Benjamin Franklin

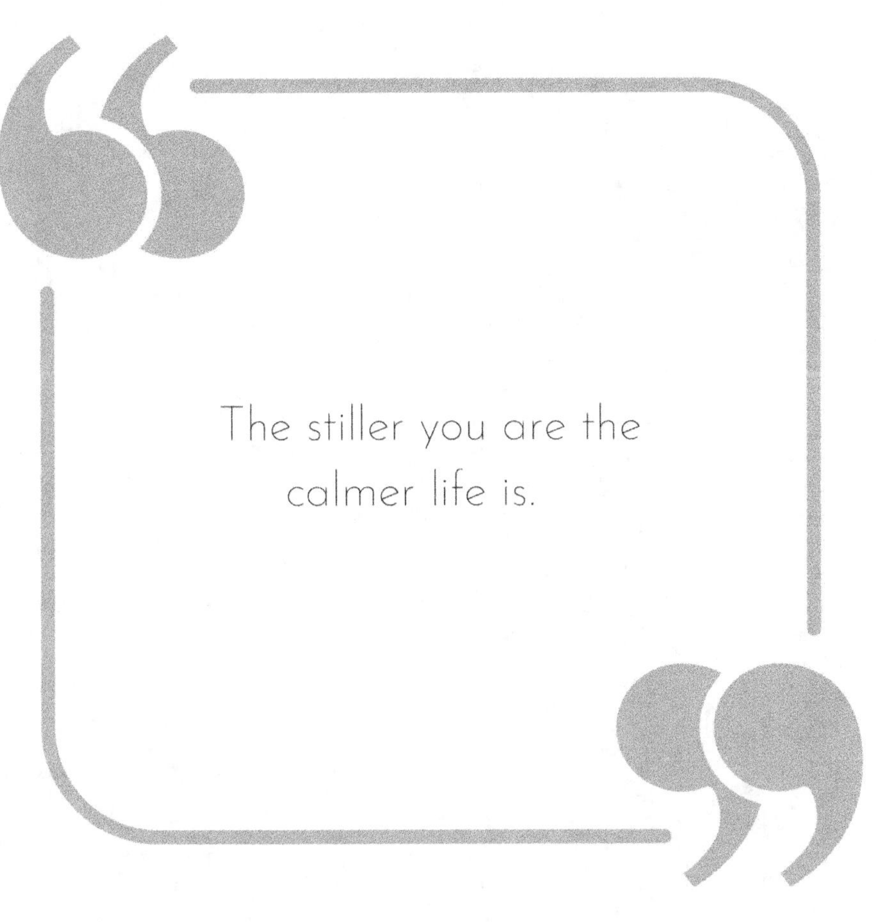

The stiller you are the
calmer life is.

Rasheed Ogunlaru

Meditation really helps create not only a sense of balance... but serenity and kind of a calm state of mind.

Eva Mendes

Many people are alive but
don't touch the miracle of
being alive.

Thich Nhat Hanh

At the end of the day, I can
end up just totally wacky,
because I've made
mountains out of molehills.
With meditation, I can keep
them as molehills.

Ringo Starr

Enjoy the little things, for
one day you may look back
and realize they were the
big things.

Robert Brault

I meditate in the morning, I have my centering, I need that. For me, training is also my meditation.

Dwayne Johnson

I thought when I started
meditation that I was going
to get real calm and peaceful
and it's going to be over. It's
not that way; it's so energetic.
That's where all the energy
and creativity is.

David Lynch

We are meant to live in joy.
This does not mean that life
will be easy and painless. It
means that we can turn our
faces to the wind and accept
that this is the storm we must
pass through.

Desmond Tutu

The whole thing about
meditation and yoga is about
connecting to the higher part
of yourself and then seeing
that every living thing is
connected in some way.

Gillian Anderson

When you're a kid, you lay in
the grass and watch the
clouds going over, and you
literally don't have a thought
in your mind. It's purely
meditation, and we lose that.

Dick Van Dyke

Peace comes from within.
Do not seek it without.

Buddha

Much of spiritual life is self-acceptance, maybe all of it.

Jack Kornfield

If your mind is empty, it is always ready for anything; it is open to everything. In the beginner's mind there are many possibilities, in the expert's mind there are few.

Shunryu Suzuki

Meditate. Slow down.
There's no rush.

Maxime Lagace

The act of meditation is
being spacious.

Sogyal Rinpoche

You cannot control the results, only your actions.

Allan Lokos

Whether you think you can
or you think you can't, you're
right.

Henry Ford

E.B. White,
Charlotte's Web

305

We cannot force the
development of mindfulness.

Allen Lokos

Nothing can harm you as
much as your own thoughts
unguarded.

Buddha

Mindful eating is a way to become reacquainted with the guidance of our internal nutritionist.

Jan Chozen Bays

I will breathe. I will think of solutions. I will not let my worry control me. I will not let my stress level break me.

Shayne McClendon

It feels good. Kind of like
when you have to shut your
computer down, just
sometimes when it goes crazy,
you just shut it down and
when you turn it on, it's okay
again. That's what meditation
is to me.

Ellen DeGeneres

There are always flowers for
those who want to see them.

Henri Matisse

Nothing ever goes away
until it has taught us what
we need to know.

Pema Chödrön

Look at other people and ask yourself if you are really seeing them or just your thoughts about them.

Jon Kabat-Zinn

If you get tired, learn to rest
not to quit.

Banksy

When I let go of what I am,
I become what I want to be.

Lao Tzu

Everything is created twice, first in the mind and then in reality.

Robin S. Sharma

Difficult roads often lead to beautiful destinations. The best is yet to come.

Zig Ziglar

The simple things are also
the most extraordinary
things, and only the wise
can see them.

Paulo Coelho, The
Alchemist

Everywhere I go, I still have time to meditate. People think meditating is sitting there, nobody bothering you, but you can even talk and still meditate.

Jet Li

There are three ways to ultimate success: The first way is to be kind. The second way is to be kind. The third way is to be kind.

Fred Rogers

Meditation allows us to deal with life as it is rather than looking at it and comparing it with how we think it's supposed to be.

Jeff Kober

The more man meditates
upon good thoughts, the
better will be his world and
the world at large.

Confucius

Love cannot be shared, it multiplies.

Agnes Ledig

The best way to meditate is
through meditation itself.

Ramana Maharshi

Don't let the noise of other opinions drown your own inner voice.

Steve Jobs

The reason why I meditate
and pray in general is just
to remind myself that it is
not about me.

Macklemore

You cannot change the
circumstances, the seasons,
or the wind, but you can
change yourself. That is
something you have.

Jim Rohn

When you listen to yourself,
everything comes naturally.
It comes from inside, like a
kind of will to do something.
Try to be sensitive.

Petri Räisänen

"You don't meditate once and suddenly your life turns around. What it does is it lets you train your brain to be able to become more stable in an action-oriented way.

Goldie Hawn

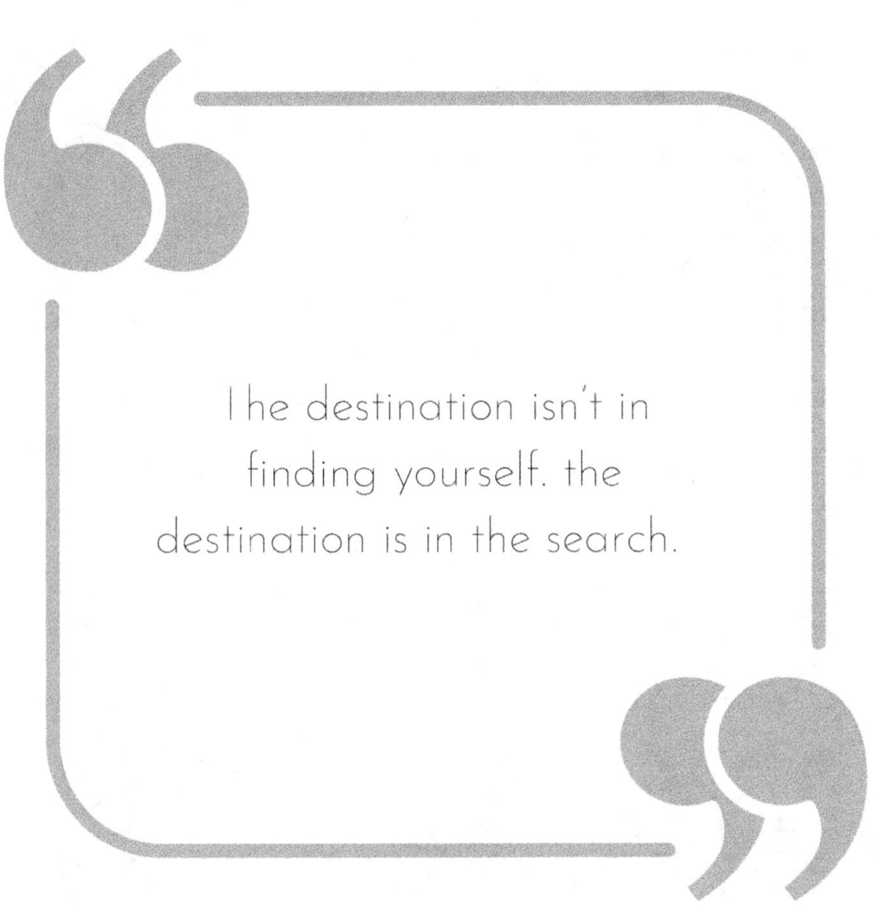

Thomas Warfield

330

We all wish for world peace, but world peace will never be achieved unless we first establish peace within our own minds.

Geshe Kelsang Gyatso

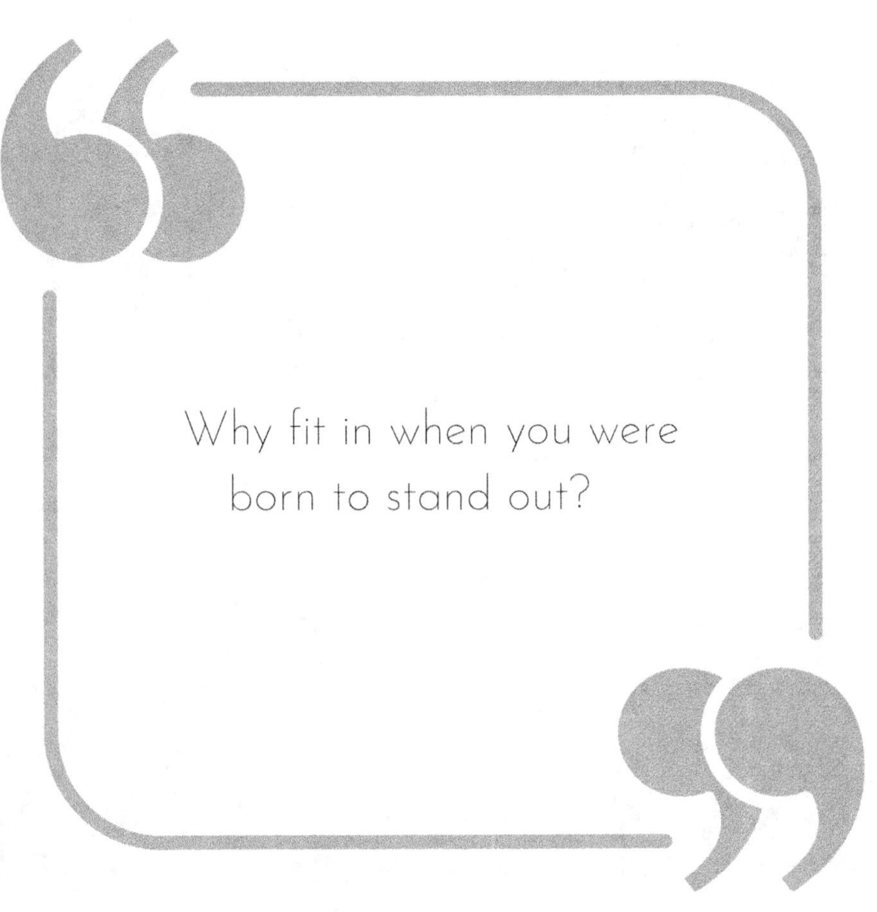

Dr. Seuss

True meditation is about being fully present with everything that is including discomfort and challenges. It is not an escape from life.

Craig Hamilton

Meditation is bringing the
mind home.

Sogyal Rinpoche

Change only happens in the present moment. The past is already done. The future is just energy and intention.

Kino MacGregor

If the ocean can calm itself,
so can you. We are both
salt water mixed with air.

Nayyirah Waheed

The body is your temple.
Keep it pure and clean for
the soul to reside in.

B.K.S Iyengar

Meditate every single day.
Not once in a while. Every
single day.

Khensu

More smiling, less worrying. More compassion, less judgment. More blessed, less stressed.

Roy T. Bennett

Go within every day and
find the inner strength so
that the world will not blow
your candle out.

Katherine Dunham

Meditation can help us
embrace our worries, our
fear, our anger; and that is
very healing. We let our
own natural capacity of
healing do the work.

Thich Nhat Hanh

Unknown

The two most powerful
warriors are patience and
time.

Leo Tolstoy,
War and Peace

Inner peace begins the moment you choose not to allow another person or event to control your emotions.

Kathryn Budig

Meditation is choosing not
to engage in the drama of
the mind but elevating the
mind to its highest potential.

Amit Ray

Travel light, live light,
spread the light, be the
light.

Yogi Bhajan

As the witnessing presence
of Awareness, we stand in
the background of
experience; as the light of
pure Knowing, we stand at
its heart.

Rupert Spira

Within you there is a
stillness and sanctuary to
which you can retreat at
any time and be yourself.

Hermann Hesse

The body benefits from movement, and the mind benefits from stillness.

Sakyong Mipham

Altogether, the idea of meditation is not to create states of ecstasy or absorption, but to experience being.

Chogyam Trungpa

"What day is it?" asked
Pooh. "It's today," squeaked
Piglet. "My favourite day,"
said Pooh.

A A Milne,
Winnie the Pooh

351

Being mindful means that we suspend judgment for a time, set aside our immediate goals for the future, and take in the present moment as it is rather than as we would like it to be.

Mark Williams

Mindfulness is a way of being present: paying attention to and accepting what is happening in our lives. It helps us to be aware of and step away from our automatic and habitual reactions to our everyday experiences.

Elizabeth Thornton

The best mediation is effortless. The best meditation is a gentle awareness.

Maxime Lagace

When you experience joy, remembering that 'This too shall pass' helps you savour the here and now. When you experience pain and sorrow, remembering that 'This too shall pass' reminds you that grief, like joy, is only temporary.

Joey Green

Every experience, no matter
how bad it seems, holds
within it a blessing of some
kind. The goal is to find it.

Buddha

Mindful eating means simply eating or drinking while being aware of each bite or sip.

Thich Nhat Hanh

This isn't just "another day, another dollar." It's more like "another day, another miracle.

Victoria Moran

When even one virtue becomes our nature, the mind becomes clean and tranquil. Then there is no need to practice meditation; we will automatically be meditating always.

Swami Satchidananda

We must experience the Truth in a direct, practical and real way. This is only possible in the stillness and silence of the mind; and this is achieved by means of meditation.

Samael Aun Weor

Be free like a balloon is. Let
go of all the weights
(negativity) to fly to the
highest of skies.

Aman Khurana

How we pay attention to the present moment largely determines the character of our experience, and therefore, the quality of our lives.

Sam Harris

Meditation is hanging out
with your soul.

Rachel Ritlop

If it's out of your hands, it
deserves freedom from your
mind, too.

Ivan Nuru

The thing about meditation
is: You become more and
more you.

David Lynch